STECK-VAUGHN

PORTRAIT OF AMERICA

Minnesota

Steck-Vaughn Company

Executive Editor	Diane Sharpe
Senior Editor	Martin S. Saiewitz
Design Manager	Pamela Heaney
Photo Editor	Margie Foster

Proof Positive/Farrowlyne Associates, Inc.
Program Editorial, Revision Development, Design, and Production

Consultant: Susan Balgie, Communications Specialist, Minnesota Office of Tourism

Published by Raintree Steck-Vaughn Publishers, an imprint of Steck-Vaughn Company.

A Turner Educational Services, Inc. book. Based on the Portrait of America television series by R. E. (Ted) Turner.

Cover Photo: Split Rock Lighthouse State Park by © Jeff Gnass/The Stock Market.

Library of Congress Cataloging-in-Publication Data

Thompson, Kathleen.
    Minnesota / Kathleen Thompson.
      p. cm. — (Portrait of America)
    "Based on the Portrait of America television series"—T.p. verso.
    "A Turner book."
    Includes index.
    ISBN 0-8114-7343-0 (library binding).—ISBN 0-8114-7448-8 (softcover)
    1. Minnesota—Juvenile literature. [1. Minnesota]. I. Series:
Thompson, Kathleen. Portrait of America.
F606.3.T48 1996
977.6—dc20

                                     95-43846
                                        CIP
                                        AC

Acknowledgments
The publishers wish to thank the following for permission to reproduce photographs:
P. 7 © Greg Ryan/Sally Beyer; p. 8 St. Paul Convention & Visitors Bureau; p. 10 Minnesota Historical Society; p. 11(top) Public Archives Canada, (middle) North Wind Picture Archives; p. 12 (top) Minnesota Office of Tourism, (bottom) Minnesota Historical Society; pp. 13 (both), 15 Minnesota Historical Society; p. 16 Lake Superior Museum of Transportation; pp. 17 (both), 18 Minnesota Historical Society; p. 19 (top) Minnesota Historical Society, (bottom) Superior National Forest; pp. 20, 21, 22 (both), 23 Courtesy The Mayo Clinic; p. 24 Minnesota Office of Tourism/St. Paul Convention & Visitors Bureau; p. 26 (top) George A. Hormel & Company, (bottom) American Dairy Association; p. 27 (top) Land O' Lakes, Inc., (bottom) © Loren Santow; p. 28 (top) Courtesy 3M, (bottom) Northshore Mining Company; p. 29 (top) © Michael Reagan, (bottom) Minnesota Office of Tourism; pp. 30 (both), 31 © Michael Reagan; pp. 32, 33 Mall of America; p. 34 Minnesota Office of Tourism; p. 36 (top) Minnesota Office of Tourism, (bottom) © Michael Reagan; pp. 37, 38 Minnesota Historical Society; p. 39 (top) Minnesota Historical Society, (bottom) © Jim Brandenburg; pp. 40, 41 Minnesota Department of Natural Resources; p. 42 © Superstock; p. 44 Minnesota Office of Tourism; p. 46 One Mile Up; p. 47 (left) One Mile Up, (center) © S. J. Lang/Vireo, (right) National Wildlife Research Center.

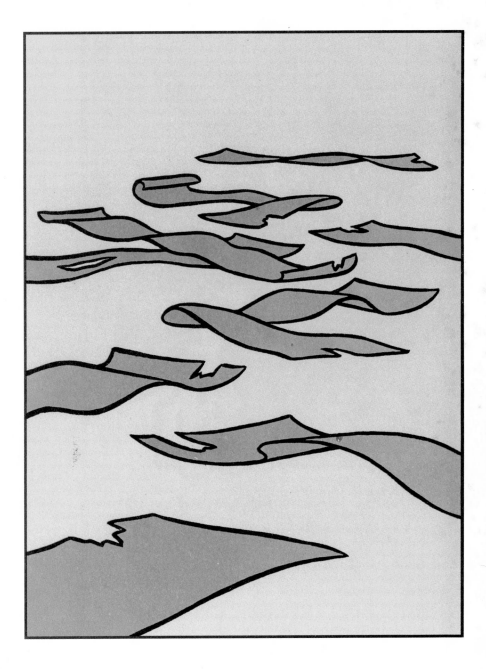

their blue ribbons, sat around
and admired themselves for
quite some time.

STECK-VAUGHN
PORTRAIT OF AMERICA

Minnesota

Kathleen Thompson

A Turner Book

RSVP
RAINTREE
STECK-VAUGHN
PUBLISHERS
The Steck-Vaughn Company

Austin, Texas

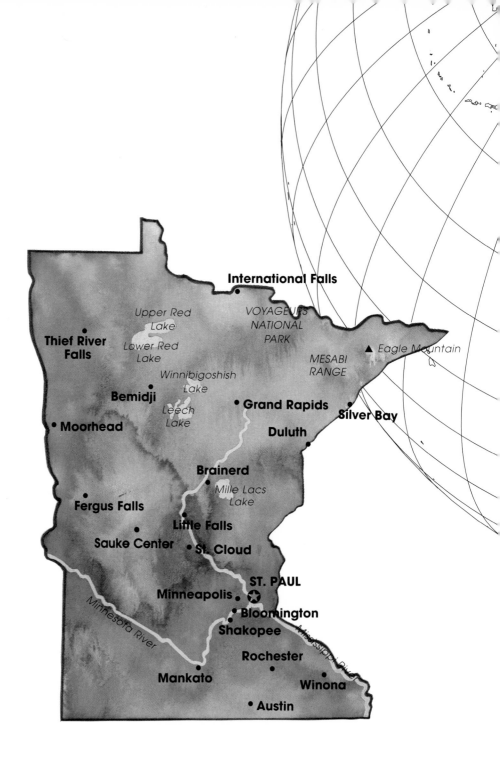

International Falls

VOYAGEURS
NATIONAL
PARK

Upper Red
Lake

Lower Red
Lake

▲ Eagle Mountain

Thief River
Falls

MESABI
RANGE

Winnibigoshish
Lake

Bemidji

Grand Rapids

Silver Bay

Leech
Lake

Duluth

Moorhead

Brainerd

Mille Lacs
Lake

Fergus Falls

Little Falls

Sauke Center

St. Cloud

ST. PAUL

Minneapolis

Bloomington

Minnesota River

Shakopee

Mississippi River

Rochester

Mankato

Winona

Austin

Minnesota

Contents

Introduction

To know Minnesota is to love the outdoors. And there's a lot of outdoors to love in Minnesota. The land of "sky-tinted waters" is the largest of the Midwestern states. Forests spread over 35 percent of the land. Thousands of sparkling inland lakes, rivers, creeks, and waterfalls splash and rush from every direction. In many ways the outdoors have made Minnesota a virtual playground. There is plenty of room for camping, swimming, hiking, boating, fishing, and hunting. And winter only adds to the variety! Minnesotans layer on the clothing and strap on skates or skis. They climb aboard snowmobiles or sail iceboats. Minnesota is a land created to experience the outdoors.

The beauty of Minnesota in the winter is displayed here, where Tettegouche State Park juts into Lake Superior.

Minnesota

Winter Festival, Populists, lakes

A Land Carved from the Forest

Archaeologists have evidence that early ancestors of Native Americans lived in present-day Minnesota about ten thousand years ago. Later civilizations left evidence of weapons carved from stone. They also left petroglyphs, which are carvings of people and animals on rock surfaces. These same people also built more than ten thousand low earth burial mounds throughout the state. They hunted animals for meat and furs and gathered berries, nuts, and other vegetation from the forests.

The Santee Sioux were the descendants of these primitive people. This group belonged to the eastern branch of the great Sioux nation, which stretched from the Great Lakes to the Rocky Mountains. They lived in permanent villages along the many lakes and rivers in the northern woodlands of present-day Minnesota. They grew corn, beans, and squash, and in the fall they harvested wild rice.

Two French fur traders, Pierre d'Esprit, Sieur de Radisson, and Médard Chouart, Sieur de Groselliers,

Native Americans carved this monument to their god of peace.

This historic painting depicts Native Americans on a buffalo hunt. In the fifteenth century, Native Americans hunted buffalo on foot until European explorers arrived with horses.

arrived in present-day Minnesota between 1654 and 1660. They explored the northwestern shore of Lake Superior, and they traded with the Santee Sioux. Other French traders followed.

The French lived in peace with the Santee and other Native American groups. The French were not interested in establishing permanent settlements. They trapped beaver and otter for their fur, traded with the Native Americans, and converted some of them to Christianity.

In 1679 the French explorer, Daniel Greysolon, Sieur du Luth, and his crew arrived on the western shore of Lake Superior at the present-day site of Duluth. He traveled through the Minnesota area in search of a route to the Pacific Ocean. Du Luth claimed the region from Lake Superior to the Mississippi River for France.

In the early 1700s, the Ojibwa, also known as the Chippewa, moved from the East into the forested northeastern section of present-day Minnesota. This move forced the Santee to relocate to the southwestern plains. The Ojibwa had been forced out of their own lands by the Iroquois, who themselves were forced out of their lands by European settlers. In 1736 the Santee wanted their land back, and bitter fighting erupted between the Ojibwa and the Santee. The two groups remained bitter enemies for many years.

The French built forts to protect the land they had claimed. The French built a fort on Lake Pepin in

southeast Minnesota in 1686. In 1700 they built another fort on the Blue Earth River, more than a hundred miles farther west. Between 1731 and 1743, they opened a canoe route for the fur trade from Lake Superior to Lake Winnipeg, 330 miles to the northwest.

In 1754 the French and the British began fighting over territory in North America. The conflict became known as the French and Indian War because most of the Native Americans supported the French against the British. The French had already claimed Canada and much of what is now the far northern United States. This area included Minnesota and the Great Lakes. The British controlled the East Coast from New England to Georgia. Each country wanted a larger portion, however.

After a few French victories, the British won most of the battles. The Treaty of Paris ended the fighting in 1763. France surrendered to Great Britain all its North American lands east of the Mississippi. This

Fur traders were the first Europeans to arrive in Minnesota. Fur hats, such as the beaver hat worn by Benjamin Franklin in this drawing, were very popular in the seventeenth and eighteenth centuries.

area included Canada as well as the northern and eastern parts of present-day Minnesota. Twenty years later, the colonists' victory against the British in the Revolutionary War established the United States. All the former French lands east of the Mississippi River and south of Canada became part of the new nation.

In 1803 President Thomas Jefferson made one of the biggest land deals in history. It was called the Louisiana Purchase. France sold the United States all the land in the Mississippi River valley for $15 million. The purchase more than doubled the size of the United States. The rest of present-day Minnesota, as well as most of the central part of the United States all the way to western Montana, became part of the United States.

Two years later Zebulon M. Pike traveled up the Mississippi River and explored central Minnesota. Then, in 1819 the United States Army began building Fort Snelling, the first permanent United States settlement in the region. It was a military fort at the point where the Mississippi and Minnesota rivers meet, just south of what are now the cities of Minneapolis and St. Paul.

Fort Snelling was the beginning of permanent settlement in present-day Minnesota. Soldiers began farming, milling flour, and cutting lumber. Fort Snelling became an important departure point for explorers and settlers traveling to the north and the west. Soon steamboats carrying supplies were traveling up the Mississippi River to the

above. The Mississippi River originates in northern Minnesota. In 1832 an explorer named Henry Schoolcraft followed it to its source at Lake Itasca.

below. An infantry drill at historic Fort Snelling is performed much as it might have been in the 1820s.

fort. Steamboats also provided an easier way for settlers to come to the region than the difficult journey over land. Besides the soldiers at the fort, many of the first settlers were French-Canadians who moved west as a result of their work in the fur trade. A few traders and missionaries also arrived via the Mississippi River.

By the 1830s, word of the region's vast forestland had reached the populations in the East. Waves of lumberworkers and their families arrived in the St. Croix Valley. Farmers and others settled in the Plains.

Buffalo and other game animals grew scarce as settlers cut down trees and converted the land into farms. Both the Santee and the Ojibwa depended on the buffalo. The Native Americans not only ate the meat, but also used the hide for blankets, robes, and coverings for their homes. By 1837 the buffalo were gone from the eastern part of Minnesota. The Native Americans were forced to sell their land to the United States government and move farther west.

More and more settlers poured into Minnesota— and they required more and more land. In 1851 the

Originally called Fort St. Anthony, Fort Snelling received its current name in 1825. The fort is shown here in 1848, when it was a center of trade and culture as well as a military outpost.

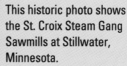

This historic photo shows the St. Croix Steam Gang Sawmills at Stillwater, Minnesota.

Santee once again were forced to move. They signed a treaty in which they sold most of their land in southern Minnesota to the United States government. About eight thousand Native Americans resettled on a narrow strip of land along the Minnesota River. The federal government promised to buy the land in a series of yearly payments. In 1854 and 1855, the Ojibwa sold almost all of the northern half of Minnesota to the government. Most of them settled on several small reservations in the area where they had once roamed freely.

Immigrants from Germany, Sweden, and Norway arrived when a land office was established in Saint Croix Falls in 1848. These immigrants started new villages and farms. Soon the small settlements became towns. On March 3, 1849, the United States government established the Territory of Minnesota. Its northern, eastern, and southern boundaries were the same as those of today, but its western limits stretched into most of what is now North Dakota. In 1857 the territory's 150,000 settlers called a convention to write a state constitution. A state constitution had to be accepted by the United States Congress before a territory could be admitted to the Union as a state. In 1858 Minnesota became the thirty-second state.

At about the same time, members of Congress were arguing about the issues of slavery and states' rights. Nearly every time a new state was admitted to the Union, Congress debated whether the state should be admitted as a "free state" or a "slave state." In 1860 Abraham Lincoln, an antislavery candidate, was elected President. Southern proslavery states withdrew from the Union and established a separate government called the Confederacy. Lincoln called on the Union states to provide soldiers to fight the Civil War that resulted from the split. Minnesota was the first state to volunteer troops.

Minnesota was far from most of the Civil War fighting, but it had trouble of another kind. Because most of the Minnesota soldiers were off fighting the Civil War, only a few were left to maintain peacekeeping efforts with Native Americans on reservations. The Santee were living on a small piece of land where they could not find enough food to eat. What's more, by 1862 the money for the 1851 land sale still had not been paid. The federal government claimed it needed every dollar to fight the Civil War. By summer the Santee were starving to death. So they fought back.

In 1862 the Santee, led by Little Crow, began to attack settlers in the Minnesota River valley. During six weeks of fierce fighting, nearly six hundred people were killed, including settlers, soldiers, and Santee. At the end of this war, 38 Santee were convicted of murder and were hanged. Hundreds more were jailed. The federal government forced the rest to leave their homes and resettle on reservations in South Dakota. The Winnebago, who had not been involved in the war in any way, were also made to leave the state. Little Crow fled from Minnesota into Canada at the end

The people in this photo had just fled from the area near New Ulm, where the Santee attacked the settlers in 1862.

The *William Crooks,* Minnesota's first railroad locomotive, went into service about 1861.

of the war. But he tried to return a year later and was killed by settlers.

By the late 1800s, farmers were growing a variety of crops, and the lumber industry had stepped up its pace. Steamboats, railroads, and highways linked Minnesota with markets around the country. In 1884 the first shipment of iron ore was made from the Vermilion Range in northeastern Minnesota. In 1890 miners extracted iron ore from the Mesabi Range in the north-central region. That area soon became the nation's largest source of iron.

An interesting thing was happening in Minnesota politics in the 1870s. The farmers did not feel they were being treated well by members of the Republican party, who were in power in the state. They also resented the high prices that railroads charged for storing and transporting crops. The farmers banded together to form an organization called the Grange. Their first major success was getting laws passed to limit the power of the railroads. By the 1890s the Populist party had grown out of the efforts of the Grange. The party represented the interests of farmers, miners, and factory workers.

As Minnesota entered the twentieth century, its magnificent natural resources began to show signs of depletion. The pine forests were almost completely gone. In addition to widespread cutting by lumber companies, a massive forest fire in 1894 had wiped out four hundred square miles of forest. Unwise farming methods made the state's farmlands less fertile every year. The iron ore was beginning to run out.

As a result Minnesota's lumber industry began producing wood pulp, a product made from smaller, younger trees. Farmers formed cooperatives, changed crops, and started using soil conservation methods. More and more Minnesotans moved to the cities and began working in manufacturing. Steel production at the U.S. Steel Corporation plant in Duluth began in 1915.

World War I, which the United States entered in 1917, also contributed to the health of Minnesota's economy. The war brought a demand for many of the state's products. Its wheat became food for the soldiers

above. In 1932 farmers harvested wheat in the Red River valley with horse-drawn reapers. The reaper was invented by Cyrus McCormick in 1834 and was the first successful harvesting machine.

below. Until nearly all the forests were cut down, lumbering was Minnesota's leading industry. This photo of a lumber camp was taken around 1885.

in Europe. The state's iron ore industry produced steel to make guns, tanks, and artillery.

Politically, the biggest change came when workers in the cities joined farmers to demand better government. A group called the Nonpartisan League was formed in 1918. Later, it was called the Farmer-Labor party. This political party demanded that the government do more for the people of the state. It called for the government to finance projects that gave farmers a better chance to make a profit on their crops and gave workers a better chance to find jobs.

These efforts helped Minnesota through the worst of the Great Depression of the 1930s. During the Depression many banks around the country lost money and were forced to close. The result was that many companies also closed, and millions of people were suddenly out of work. Prices skyrocketed, and few people could afford the things they used to buy.

However, World War II brought prosperity to Minnesota, as it did to most states. The United States entered the war in 1941. Once again Minnesota's wheat and iron ore were vital to the war effort. As factories reopened, many people left the farms and moved to the cities to find work.

In 1944 the Farmer-Labor party joined with the Democratic party to form the Democratic Farmer-Labor party (DFL). In 1948 the DFL elected Hubert Humphrey to the United States Senate. Humphrey was elected Vice President of the United States in 1964. Walter F. Mondale, another Minnesotan, was elected to the same office 12 years later.

During the Great Depression, Floyd B. Olson was the first of three Farmer-Labor governors whose progressive policies helped Minnesota workers and farmers.

By 1950 the state's supply of high-grade iron ore was almost depleted. But deposits of lower-grade taconite—rock containing twenty to thirty percent iron—had been discovered. Economical methods of refining taconite were developed. A huge processing plant was opened at Silver Bay, on the coast of Lake Superior north of Duluth. For a while, Minnesota's mining was revived. In the 1980s, however, low-cost iron ore and processed steel from abroad were replacing taconite and steel made in the United States.

A more permanent boost to the state's economy was the opening of the St. Lawrence Seaway in 1959. This 23,000-mile-long waterway links the Great Lakes to the Atlantic Ocean via the St. Lawrence River. Duluth, at the western tip of Lake Superior, is the western end of this great water route. Since the seaway opened, Duluth has become a major international port. Today, it is the largest freshwater port in the world.

Preservation of natural resources is a major issue in Minnesota. In the 1970s and 1980s, Minnesota forced mining companies to cease polluting the air and the water, especially Lake Superior. In addition, huge amounts of land are now protected by the state to ensure that the beauty of Minnesota will last well into the future.

above. Minnesota farmers brought a cow and a horse to the state capitol in the 1930s to dramatize their demand for relief.

below. Today, lumber companies can only cut down trees of a certain age. Workers extract thin wood rods and count the ring marks to determine a tree's age.

A Family Medical History

After graduating from the University of Missouri, Dr. William Mayo moved to Minnesota and began practicing medicine in 1855. He soon earned a very good reputation as a skilled surgeon. Dr. Mayo was known for being willing to try new methods for improving health care. For example, he was one of the first doctors in the West to use a microscope to find the cause of illness. Dr. Mayo was also active in his community. In 1862 fight-ing between the Sioux and some settlers left hundreds of people dead or injured. Dr. Mayo spent many long hours volunteering his skills as a surgeon during this time.

In 1863 Dr. Mayo opened a small clinic in Rochester, a small farming community about 85 miles southeast of Minneapolis and St. Paul. Many of his patients were farmers. In addition to the usual illnesses found in any community, the farmers presented greater challenges. Sometimes one of them got a hand or a foot caught in a piece of farm machinery. When this happened, there was nothing a doctor of that time could do but cut off the injured limb. Then the patient either recovered or died. Many died because at that time no one understood that germs cause infections. So sterilization and disinfecting techniques that we take for granted today were not used. As many as forty percent of Dr. Mayo's patients who were operated on died.

In 1869 Dr. Mayo visited New York and Pennsylvania to learn the latest surgical skills and techniques. He assisted a number of doctors in surgical procedures, working with the newest equipment and discussing new

Dr. William W. Mayo, a country physician, settled in Rochester in 1863.

techniques was the process of disinfecting. Charles learned the importance of disinfecting the instruments before surgery as well as the wound afterward. After he graduated in 1888, Charles Mayo brought these techniques to Rochester.

William Mayo, Sr., in the meantime, was working at a temporary hospital in Rochester. It had been built to assist the victims of a cyclone that had ripped through the community. In 1889 a permanent hospital, called St. Mary's Hospital, was built and Dr. William Mayo, Sr., became chief of staff. His sons later joined him as part of the St. Mary's medical team. And Charles brought the amazing breakthrough of disinfecting techniques with him.

Ordinarily, medical breakthroughs such as this would not reach small farm communities for many years. So the patients of St. Mary's were especially fortunate. The recovery rates of patients at St. Mary's improved greatly

ideas. This kind of hands-on experience was very valuable. He made other such trips whenever he could afford the time and money.

Meanwhile, his sons—William, Jr., and Charles—were getting ready to enter medical school. Later, the three planned to form a family medical clinic. Of the three, it was perhaps Charles who learned the most valuable lesson.

Charles Mayo entered Chicago Medical College in 1885. At that time modern medical doctors still did not understand the role of germs in infections. The Chicago Medical College, however, taught Charles modern techniques from Europe. One of these

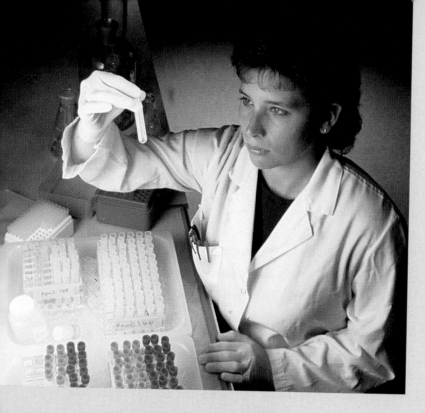

after the Mayos began using the disinfecting techniques. Soon the father-and-sons team was famous throughout the Midwest.

In 1905 the brothers opened the Mayo Clinic. Together with the University of Minnesota, in 1915 Charles and William established the Mayo Graduate School of Medicine. The brothers set up the nation's first blood bank in 1933. In 1950 Mayo Clinic scientists won the Nobel Prize for developing the drug cortisone.

Today, the Mayo Clinic includes more than a dozen buildings and two hospital complexes. The governing organization, called the Mayo Foundation, also operates three medical schools, laboratories, a

The Plummer building, built in 1928, now houses medical offices and services associated with the Mayo Clinic.

publishing house, and seven branch facilities in five states. It employs almost 22,000 people and treats 400,000 patients a year.

From the very beginning, the first Dr. Mayo charged people only what they could afford to pay. The Mayo Clinic has a similar policy; it operates as a nonprofit organization. Any money the clinic earns beyond its expenses is put into medical research and expansion.

The Mayo Clinic still makes it a policy to bring the latest in medical knowledge and technology to health care. Through video satellite links, doctors at the clinic now can examine X rays and join examinations of patients who are thousands of miles away. Dr. William Mayo, Sr., would probably be amazed if he could see this modern technique. But with his famous desire for the best in patient care, he no doubt would approve.

The Mayo Clinic maintains a fleet of helicopters and planes. The clinic will pick up patients in emergency situations.

Land of Peace and Plenty

When European settlers arrived in present-day Minnesota, they found a land with plenty of everything. There was an abundance of fur-bearing animals, such as beaver and otter. Great stands of trees swept across the northern half of the area. There was plenty of good, rich soil and water for crops. The lakes and rivers teemed with a wide variety of fish. Later, iron ore was discovered. It seemed that the natural wealth of this land would never run out.

During the early 1800s, fur trading was the area's principal source of revenue. A trapper could earn great wealth by trapping all winter and trading the furs for gold and supplies in the spring. Eventually extensive trapping made the fur-bearing animals scarce.

Lumber took over as Minnesota's major industry beginning in the early 1800s. A large number of trees were cut down and sent to sawmills. There the logs were converted into lumber for use by Minnesota's growing population and for shipment to cities in the East. Soon it was clear that the lumber industry would

The Landmark Center, St. Paul's performing arts complex, was built in an old courthouse in 1978. The construction was part of renovations in the downtown area that were intended to give new life to the city's economy.

eventually strip the land of all its trees. They could not continue to cut down trees without also planting new ones. The lumber companies began reforesting the land. Today, about a third of Minnesota is covered with forests. Most of this is state or federal land, so the lumber companies must comply with strict government regulations. These restrictions make lumbering less profitable, but they ensure that there will always be forests in Minnesota.

These days, Minnesota's number one farm product is dairy goods. After that, in order, come beef cattle, soybeans, hogs, corn, wheat, turkeys, and sugar beets. Minnesota is the nation's leading producer of sugar beets, and it is the second largest producer of turkeys and sweet corn. It ranks third in dairy products, soybeans, and hogs. Minnesota also has many apple orchards. Various fruits and vegetables are grown on farms around the state.

Manufacturing passed agriculture as the state's leading industry around 1952. Today, manufacturing accounts for more than $20 billion in income for the

Dairy products are Minnesota's most valuable agricultural output. The state ranks third in the United States in dairy production.

26

Food processing is a major industry in Minnesota. This is a cheese-processing plant in Perham.

state. Most of Minnesota's manufacturing income is generated by companies making industrial machinery, especially computers. Successful computer companies, such as Cray Research, Unisys, and IBM, have major manufacturing facilities in Minnesota.

Companies in Minnesota also manufacture scientific instruments and measuring and control devices, such as thermostats. The state also has several large defense contractors and weapons manufacturers.

The state's second largest manufacturing industry is food products. Minnesota's food-processing plants pack meat and poultry, can vegetables, refine sugar beets, process soybean oil, make malt liquors, and turn raw milk into a wide range of dairy foods. Minnesota's food-processing companies, such as Pillsbury, General Mills, and Land O' Lakes, are names that are recognized in supermarkets throughout the country.

Paper products are the third most profitable segment of Minnesota's manufacturing industry. Paper companies can use younger and smaller trees than those needed for lumber. They can also use faster-growing trees that have softer wood. So today, the

These workers at General Mills, one of Minnesota's chief food processors, help to produce Cheerios.

27

Headquartered in St. Paul, 3M is a $15 billion manufacturing company with operations in 61 countries. 3M produces sixty thousand paper products, including Post-it notes, sandpaper, and Scotch Magic tape.

major product of Minnesota's vast forests is not lumber. Rather, it is almost every kind of paper product you can think of.

With all that paper being made, you might expect Minnesota to have a vigorous printing and publishing industry, and you'd be right. Several book publishers are located in the state. Metal products, including guns and ammunition, are another large manufacturing area.

As Minnesota's once-great iron ore reserves have dwindled, mining has become a less important part of the state's economy. Today, mining contributes less than one percent of the state's earnings. Still, about three quarters of the iron ore mined in the United States comes from Minnesota. Granite, limestone, clay, sand, and gravel are also mined in the state.

Minnesota also has a healthy fishing industry. Fishermen catch and sell fish both from Lake Superior and from the thousands of inland lakes. In addition,

This aerial view is of a metal-processing plant called an iron range. After iron is mined, it must be processed to separate it from other minerals.

The mythical logger Paul Bunyan is a heroic figure in Minnesota tall tales. These statues of Paul Bunyan and Babe, his blue ox, attract tourists to Bemidji.

access to the Great Lakes by way of Lake Superior has made Minnesota a transportation and distribution center for products made in other Upper Midwest states.

Lastly, Minnesota's income from tourism has risen steadily. More and more people are discovering the charm of its cities and the quiet beauty of its lush woods and sparkling lakes and streams. Trails for hiking and, in winter, for snow-mobiling and cross-country skiing wind through the many state parks and recreation areas. Visitors spend nearly $5 billion in the state every year. They've found, just as the explorers and settlers had three centuries earlier, that Minnesota is a land of peace and plenty.

This aerial photo shows the linked lakes and rivers that form Voyageurs National Park. During Minnesota's early fur-trading days, these water routes were the "main highways" through the area.

A Gift from the Gods

This Ojibwa woman has participated in wild rice harvests for nearly fifty years.

Ed Fairbanks belongs to the Native American group called the Ojibwa. For centuries the Ojibwa have harvested one special food. It is wild rice, a grain that grows in the shallow waters on the edges of clear northern lakes. Wild rice is a major part of the traditional Ojibwa diet. But the grain holds more significance than that for the Ojibwa. It forms the center of their culture and even their spirituality.

"We gather the wild rice for the same reason the fox chases the rabbit," Ed Fairbanks explains. "Whether it's for food, sport, or . . . necessity, whatever it is, it's an absolute need to do.

"It's part of us. Our religious men tell us that wild rice is an Indian. One day, the Anashanabi were hungry and they had nothing to eat. And this Indian did a dance and prayed to the Great Spirit. And he knew what he had to do. And he entered the water

When the canoes reach shore, the harvesters load the fresh rice into bags.

and his body became the rice. And that's what it is, it's an Indian. And you have to [eat] of it to live and prosper. And you have to show it that respect, just as you would your brother."

The Ojibwa pay respect by letting some of the rice they gather fall back into the water. That rice is the seed for future harvests. They also offer the very first rice from every harvest to the Great Spirit. This shows their gratitude to the gods for providing them with this plentiful and nourishing food.

Ed Fairbanks is a member of the Leech Lake Band of Ojibwa. They live on the Leech Lake Reservation, one of seven Ojibwa reservations in northern Minnesota. The reservation is about two hundred miles north of Minneapolis. It covers 920 square miles and contains 195 lakes. Two of these lakes are each more than one hundred square miles in area, with many little bays where the rice grows.

About sixty percent of the Ojibwa living there work to harvest the rice in August and September. This work is mostly done in the traditional way, from canoes by the women. While one woman guides the canoe, a second bends the tops of the rice stalks over the side of the canoe. She beats the stalks with a stick, and the kernels of rice fall into the canoe. Back at the village, the kernels are dried and husked. Leech Lake wild rice is sold throughout the United States.

There are other ways the Ojibwa make their living in these modern times. But the tradition of harvesting the wild rice remains important to them.

"It's the only time that we here on the reservation are able to do something together with Mother Nature and get that old feeling of completeness. That's what it means to us."

In the shallow water, the wild rice grows so tall and thick that it almost completely hides the Ojibwa canoe.

Megamall Comes to Minnesota

Where in the world can you find gardens and waterfalls, a giant amusement park, an aquarium, a miniature golf course, and hundreds of places to shop? They're all at the Mall of America! The list of what's there goes on and on . . . restaurants, a space exhibit, 14 movie theaters, even a wedding chapel!

Mall of America is the largest indoor retail and entertainment center in the United States. It is located in Bloomington, a five-minute drive from the Minneapolis/St. Paul International Airport. It's ten miles from both downtown Minneapolis and downtown St. Paul.

Millions of people have come to the Mall of America since it opened in August 1992. Visitors arrive from all over the world. For most people, the mention of a mall means shopping. There certainly are plenty of places to shop—about four hundred stores, carts, and kiosks. But shopping is only part of what the Mall is about. Entertainment greets visitors at almost every turn.

The Mall is in the shape of a square. Knott's Camp Snoopy is at the center. Visitors can ride the roller coaster or Ferris wheel, or they might

The Mall of America was built on the site of a former baseball stadium. Knott's Camp Snoopy, in the middle of the mall, now occupies the former playing field.

Children enjoy the Red Baron ride at Knott's Camp Snoopy, the largest indoor theme park in the United States.

stroll on scenic paths that capture the feeling of Minnesota's northwoods. Nearby is Golf Mountain, a two-level "mountain" that's part of an 18-hole miniature golf course.

Four multilevel shopping streets surround Knott's Camp Snoopy. Each street has a different theme and color scheme to help visitors find their way. The streets are called South Avenue, East Broadway, North Garden, and West Market.

Stores and restaurants use special themes to attract attention. Shoppers who stop to watch a video or listen to music near a shop might stroll inside. One popular eatery has a simulated rain forest, with plants and "animals," rainfall, and even the sound of thunder.

Just how large is the Mall of America? Imagine a huge sports arena such as Yankee Stadium. Now multiply that by seven! The Mall, in fact, was built on land where Minnesota's Metropolitan Stadium once stood.

Megamall is a word that may not appear in your dictionary. But don't be surprised if it does someday. It's a word people use to describe the Mall of America.

Clean and Easy Living

For years Garrison Keillor has been one of the most popular radio personalities in the United States. He is from Minnesota, and his special programs are done as though they are coming from the imaginary town of Lake Wobegon, Minnesota. Here is how he described the Minnesota tradition of building a 15-story, fairy-tale palace out of thirty thousand blocks of ice:

"It's not a bad idea," he said slyly. "Four hundred people could choose a worse thing to do with their time. It's something that Minnesotans seldom do anymore—building something that is so fanciful and big. . . . Minnesota suffers from an excess of sensibleness sometimes."

When you think about it, Keillor was right. Building a huge palace from ice is a wonderfully *unsen*sible thing to do. After all, it will only melt in the warmth of the spring sun! On the other hand, perhaps the palace shows just how sensible Minnesotans really are. They know that all the ice and snow that accumulates in Minnesota every winter is good for something.

The Spoonbridge and Cherry fountain is part of the Minneapolis Sculpture Garden. With forty works, the Minneapolis Sculpture Garden is the largest urban sculpture garden in the United States.

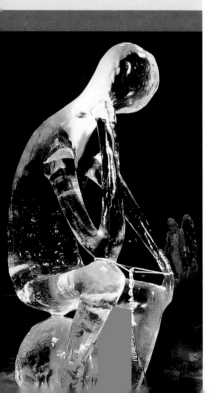

above. Cross-country skiing in the beautiful north woods is one of Minnesota's many attractions.

below. Ice sculpting is one of more than eighty events at the annual St. Paul Winter Carnival.

Rather than let it go to waste, Minnesotans put that precipitation to good use at the St. Paul Winter Carnival. The carnival is one of the nation's oldest winter festivals. There are eighty indoor and outdoor events during the two-week festival. Among these are speed-skating races, motorcycle races on ice, fireworks, and a sleigh and cutter parade. There are also ice carving and snow sculpting competitions.

The St. Paul Winter Carnival is a good example of Minnesota culture. It shows that Minnesotans love and appreciate their environment. This is also evident in the state's efforts to establish natural wildlife refuges. The Boundary Waters Canoe Area in northeastern Minnesota is a place where Minnesotans can take part fully in the natural outdoors. Outdoor activities, such as canoeing, cross-country skiing, fishing, and camping, are popular recreations there and elsewhere in the state.

Minnesota can claim to have inspired some notable writers, also. A few of these have made a lasting impression on the world of literature.

Sinclair Lewis was the first United States writer to win the Nobel Prize for literature. His novels are critical of life in small-town America. He portrayed its citizens as narrow-minded, self-satisfied, and overly concerned with making money. The setting of one of his novels, *Main Street*, is a town called Gopher Prairie, which is modeled on Sauk Centre, Minnesota.

F. Scott Fitzgerald is another great writer from Minnesota. He is best known for his novels about the Jazz Age, which took place in America in the 1920s. In his novels and short stories, Fitzgerald described the sadness and the sense of relief that swept over the United States after World War I.

Bob Dylan, a young songwriter from Minnesota, became the voice of dissatisfied youth in the 1960s. He used clever lyrics and a unique musical style to sing out against injustice and inequality.

There is no cultural category for Garrison Keillor. Like a folk singer, with an easy and relaxed style, Keillor might be labeled a "folk personality." In fact people like him because he's just plain ol' folks. For years his radio show, "A Prairie Home Companion," brought a delightful mixture of music and humor to the airwaves. He still broadcasts several programs a year. Keillor tells funny stories of life in Lake Wobegon, recites poetry, and sings songs. He also introduces a number of guest comedians, singers, and musicians who perform with him or on their own. Through it all Keillor's gentle manner delivers a message that embraces love, steadfastness, and companionship. In mythical Lake Wobegon, he claims in his warmly humorous way, "all the women are strong, all the men are good looking, and all the children are above average."

Minnesotans do not fail to enjoy the fine arts. The Twin Cities of Minneapolis and St. Paul are cultural

Sinclair Lewis won the Pulitzer Prize in 1926 for his novel *Arrowsmith*.

F. Scott Fitzgerald spent his childhood in Minnesota, but as an adult he lived in New York, Hollywood, and Europe.

centers of the northern Midwest. The Guthrie Theater in Minneapolis is internationally known as one of the nation's finest theaters for the performing arts. Nearly sixty other live theater troupes perform in the Twin Cities, as well. Among them is the Minneapolis Children's Theatre Company. This institution provides professional training to children who wish to pursue a career in acting.

Across the Mississippi River in St. Paul, the Ordway Music Theatre is home to a wide variety of performing groups. The Minnesota Orchestra, the St. Paul Chamber Orchestra, and the Minnesota Opera all perform there. And many visiting musical artists make the Ordway a "must stop" on their tours.

The visual arts are well represented in Minnesota, too. The Minneapolis Institute of Arts is a large museum with a high-quality collection of paintings and sculpture. The city also is home to the Walker Art Center, a showcase for modern art. In the summer its pleasant outdoor sculpture garden is a popular place to stroll and relax. In St. Paul the Science Museum of Minnesota makes the wonders of modern science and technology appealing and understandable through exhibits and demonstrations.

Many of Minnesota's most popular attractions deal with the state's history, particularly its pioneer life. Just south of the Twin Cities, a reconstructed Fort Snelling shows what life was like nearly two hundred years ago. Costumed performers there demonstrate many of the skills needed for survival in 1820s Minnesota. Near Shakopee, a few miles to the southwest, Murphy's

Landing is a re-creation of an 1840–1890s pioneer village. It includes reproductions of farms, a Native American village, and a fur trader's cabin. In Grand Rapids in the northern part of the state, visitors find the Forest History Center. This is a museum that tells the story of the Minnesota north woods from the time of the earliest people to the present. The center also has reconstructed a logging camp dating from the late 1800s.

The city of Duluth has several notable museums of its own. The Canal Park Marine Museum shows the history of commercial shipping in the upper Great Lakes. Also, the early days of railroading are celebrated in the Lake Superior Museum of Transportation. There visitors can walk around and sit in old railroad cars.

In Minnesota, as everywhere, the culture of a place reflects the lifestyle of the people. It shows what the people value and how they entertain themselves. A large part of Minnesota's culture is linked to its natural resources, not only because Minnesotans love outdoor activities but also because of the value they place on preserving those resources.

Abolitionist Jane Grey Swisshelm worked to end slavery and promoted women's rights during the early nineteenth century.

Garrison Keillor's radio show, "A Prairie Home Companion," features many guest artists and sometimes audience participation.

A Haven for Nature's Wonders

The Boundary Waters Canoe Area is an amazing place. It was formed more than three billion years ago when ancient volcanoes forced lava upward out of the sea. Wind and water battered the new land. Then glaciers overtook it. At the end of the Ice Age, when the glaciers receded, they uncovered a watery wilderness that was ideal for pine forests and wildlife.

Native Americans who lived in this wilderness traveled mostly by canoe through miles of lakes and rivers. They hunted the plentiful wildlife and fished the teeming waters.

When European settlers came to the area, they also traveled mostly by canoe. They spent years exploring the confusing maze of lakes and rivers. Then they began mining, logging, fishing, trapping, and settling the land.

Much later, as the land became more populated, people began to get concerned about preserving it. In the 1960s conservationists convinced the United States Forest Service to set aside the wilderness that remained. Over time the government quietly bought some of the settled land in the area, as well. Today, the Boundary Waters Canoe Area extends for about 150 miles along the northern border of the United States. Combined with Quetico Provincial Park, just beyond the international boundary into Canada, the uninterrupted wilderness totals 1.15 million acres!

Campers in the Boundary Waters Canoe Area are encouraged to practice "low-impact camping." That means they travel quietly, burn or remove any materials they bring in, and set up tents in previously used spots.

Together, these two areas provide a glimpse of North America before it was logged, mined, and "developed." On a camping trip in the Boundary Waters Canoe Area, you can leave modern life behind and watch beavers—or bears—at play. You can see flycatchers and sparrowhawks darting through the trees. And if you keep your eyes open, you might find deer browsing among the pine trees, wolves hunting prey, and loons flying overhead.

The Boundary Waters Canoe Area also offers the chance to test your skill, stamina, and strength. To travel this wilderness, you have to do more than set up a tent. You also must pack everything you need into a canoe. You have to paddle for hours at a time and then portage—or carry your pack and canoe—over patches of land between waterways.

In exchange for this hard work, you reap some great rewards. You can swim in clean, pure water, catch and cook your own fish, gaze upon billions of stars, and experience the wilderness firsthand.

The Boundary Waters Canoe Area is often called the "Canoe Capital of the World."

The Future Is Now

In many ways Minnesota is a state that is coming into its own. Its people have been working for years to create a high quality of life. They have steadily rejected what they did not like and developed what they felt they needed. This shows in the state's progressive politics, its excellent educational system, and its care for the environment.

Minnesota had its first environmental crisis almost a hundred years ago. It had lost nearly all its forestland. Clear-cutting, in which lumber companies cut down every single tree in an area, had left the land bare.

Minnesotans replanted their forests and began regulating the lumber companies. They set aside huge areas of land that would be entirely free from lumbering. Today, Minnesota's natural beauty is one of its great attractions. The state has two huge national forests, 66 state parks, and 55 state forests. In northern Minnesota, mile after mile of majestic trees provide a sheltered home to a variety of animals, plants, and other creatures.

Like many other cities, Minneapolis has redeveloped its downtown area. Many new apartment buildings and office centers, as well as a new mall, grace its skyline.

Split Rock Lighthouse, on Lake Superior north of Duluth, is the nation's highest lighthouse above the water level.

Minnesotans have always been willing to do the two things necessary for solving problems—think creatively and work hard. That willingness has made the quality of life in the state very high. Today, people all over the country recognize the importance of living in such a place. Many people believe that respect for environment and good government are more important than just high salaries. In Minnesota that sort of thinking has been fashionable since the turn of the century. As a result Minnesota has been successful in attracting new businesses. By sticking to what it believes, Minnesota seems well prepared to take its good life into the future.

Important Historical Events

1650s The Santee Sioux occupy what would become present-day Minnesota.

1654 Pierre d'Esprit, Sieur de Radisson, and Médard Chouart, Sieur de Groselliers, are the first Europeans to enter the area.

1679 Daniel Greysolon, Sieur du Luth, lands on the western shore of Lake Superior.

1680 Father Louis Hennepin discovers the Falls of St. Anthony, near Minneapolis.

1736 The Ojibwa and the Sioux battle over the northeastern section of Minnesota.

1763 The Treaty of Paris, ending the French and Indian War, gives northern and eastern Minnesota to the British.

1783 A treaty between Great Britain and the United States gives eastern Minnesota to the Americans.

1803 The Louisiana Purchase gives the rest of Minnesota to the United States.

1805 Zebulon Pike makes a treaty with the Sioux for land on which to build Fort Snelling.

1832 Henry Schoolcraft discovers the true source of the Mississippi River at Lake Itasca.

1851 The Sioux agree to a treaty giving up large parts of their land to settlement.

1854 The Ojibwa agree to treaties giving up large parts of their land to settlement.

1858 Minnesota becomes the thirty-second state.

1862 The Sioux wage war against settlers in the Minnesota River valley.

1867 A railroad from Chicago to St. Paul is opened.

1870s The Grange movement succeeds in getting laws passed to regulate the railroads.

1890 Iron ore is extracted from the Mesabi Range in the north-central region.

1918 The Nonpartisan League, later the Farmer-Labor party, is organized.

1922 A Farmer-Labor candidate is elected to the United States Senate.

1930 Minnesota writer Sinclair Lewis becomes the first United States writer to win the Nobel Prize for literature.

1931 Floyd B. Olson is elected governor.

1944 The Democratic and Farmer-Labor parties combine to form the DFL.

1948 DFL candidate Hubert Humphrey is elected to the United States Senate.

1964 Humphrey is elected Vice President of the United States.

1972 The DFL gains a majority in both houses of the legislature for the first time.

1976 Walter Mondale is elected Vice President of the United States.

1980 The Reserve Mining Company of Silver Bay complies with state supreme court rulings and stops dumping waste into Lake Superior.

1988 The worst drought since the 1930s brings disaster to farmers.

1993 Heavy spring and summer rains cause severe flooding of the Mississippi and other rivers. Nearly half of Minnesota's counties are declared disaster areas.

Minnesota's state flag is royal blue bordered with gold fringe. In the center is the state seal, surrounded by a wreath of the state flower. Nineteen stars ring the wreath. The largest star represents Minnesota, the nineteenth state to join the Union. On the seal are symbols of agriculture and lumbering. A Native American represents their contribution to the state's heritage.

Minnesota Almanac

Nickname. The Gopher State

Capital. St. Paul

State Bird. Common loon

State Flower. Pink and white lady's slipper

State Tree. Norway pine

State Motto. *L'Etoile du Nord* (The Star of the North)

State Song. "Hail! Minnesota"

State Abbreviations. Minn. (traditional); MN (postal)

Statehood. May 11, 1858, the 32nd state

Government. Congress: U.S. senators, 2; U.S. representatives, 8. State Legislature: senators, 67; representatives, 134. Counties: 87

Area. 84,397 sq mi (218,587 sq km), 12th in size among the states

Greatest Distances. north/south, 407 mi (655 km); east/west, 360 mi (580 km). Shoreline: 180 mi (290 km)

Elevation. Highest: Eagle Mountain, 2,301 ft (701 m). Lowest: 602 ft (183 m) along Lake Superior

Population. 1990 Census: 4,387,029 (8% increase over 1980), 20th among the states. Density: 52 persons per sq mi (20 persons per sq km). Distribution: 70% urban, 30% rural. 1980 Census: 4,075,970

Economy. *Agriculture*: dairy goods, beef, soybeans, hogs, corn, wheat, turkeys, sugar beets, apples, vegetables. *Fishing*: catfish, pike, carp, lake trout. *Manufacturing*: computers, scientific instruments, measuring and control devices, food products, paper products, printed materials, fabricated metal products, lumber and wood products, nonelectrical machinery, chemicals. *Mining*: iron ore, sand, gravel, granite, limestone, clay, peat

State Seal

State Bird: Common loon

State Flower: Pink and white lady's slipper

Annual Events

★ Bemidji Polar Daze (January)

★ John Beargrease Sled Dog Race north from Duluth (January)

★ Winter Carnival in St. Paul (January/February)

★ Cinco de Mayo in St. Paul (May)

★ Fiesta Days in Montevideo (June)

★ Aquatennial in Minneapolis (July)

★ Lumberjack Days in Stillwater (July)

★ Song of Hiawatha Pageant in Pipestone (July/August)

★ State Fair in St. Paul (August/September)

★ Oktoberfest in New Ulm (October)

Places to Visit

★ Boundary Waters Canoe Area in far northeastern Minnesota

★ Fort Snelling, near Minneapolis

★ Grand Portage National Monument in far northeastern Minnesota

★ Guthrie Theater in Minneapolis

★ High Falls, on the Pigeon River

★ Lumbertown, U.S.A., in Brainerd

★ Minneapolis Institute of Arts in Minneapolis

★ Pipestone National Monument, near Pipestone

★ Science Museum of Minnesota in St. Paul

★ Sibley House in Mendota

★ Statues of Paul Bunyan and Babe the Blue Ox in Bemidji

★ Voyageurs National Park in far north-central Minnesota

★ Walker Art Center in Minneapolis

3 0060 0002476 9